TRAILBLAZERS of the MODERN WORLD

HENRY FORD

By Michael Burgan

WORLD ALMANAC® LIBRARY

Please visit our web site at: www.worldalmanaclibrary.com
For a free color catalog describing World Almanac® Library's
list of high-quality books and multimedia programs,
call 1-800-848-2928 or fax your request to (414) 332-3567.

Library of Congress Cataloging-in-Publication Data

Burgan, Michael.
  Henry Ford / by Michael Burgan.
    p. cm. — (Trailblazers of the modern world)
  Includes bibliographical references and index.
  Summary: A biography of the man responsible for mass-producing the automobile in the early part of the twentieth century.
  ISBN 0-8368-5070-X (lib. bdg.)
  ISBN 0-8368-5230-3 (softcover)
  1. Ford, Henry, 1863-1947—Juvenile literature. 2. Automobile industry and trade—United States—Biography—Juvenile
literature. 3. Industrialists—United States—Biography—Juvenile literature. 4. Automobile engineers—United States—
Biography—Juvenile literature. [1. Ford, Henry, 1863-1947. 2. Industrialists. 3. Automobile industry and trade—
Biography.] I. Title. II. Series.
TL140.F6B87   2002
338.7'6292'092—dc21
  [B]   2001045627

This North American edition first published in 2002 by
World Almanac® Library
330 West Olive Street, Suite 100
Milwaukee, WI 53212 USA

This U.S. edition © 2002 by World Almanac® Library.

An Editorial Directions book
Editor: Lucia Raatma
Designer and page production: Ox and Company
Photo researcher: Dawn Friedman
Indexer: Tim Griffin
World Almanac® Library art direction: Tammy Gruenewald
World Almanac® Library production: Susan Ashley and Jessica L. Yanke

Photo credits: AP/Wide World Photos, cover; Hulton Archive/Scott Swanson Collection, 4; Collections of Henry Ford
Museum and Greenfield Village, 5; Hulton Archive, 6; Collections of Henry Ford Museum and Greenfield Village, 7 left,
7 right, 8; Hulton Archive, 9 top, Burton Historical Collection/Detroit Public Library, 9 bottom; Collections of Henry
Ford Museum and Greenfield Village, 10, 11 top; Hulton Archive, 11 bottom; Collections of Henry Ford Museum and
Greenfield Village, 12; Hulton Archive, 13; Collections of Henry Ford Museum and Greenfield Village, 14; Hulton
Archive, 15; Corbis/Bettmann, 16; Collections of Henry Ford Museum and Greenfield Village, 17, 18; AP/Wide World
Photos, 19 top; Collections of Henry Ford Museum and Greenfield Village, 19 bottom, 20 top; Hulton Archive, 20
bottom; Collections of Henry Ford Museum and Greenfield Village, 22; Hulton Archive/Stock Montage, 23 top; Hulton
Archive, 23 bottom; Collections of Henry Ford Museum and Greenfield Village, 24, 25, 26, 27, 28, 30, 31, 32; AP/Wide
World Photos, 33; Hulton Archive, 34; AP/Wide World Photos, 36; Hulton Archive, 37; Corbis/Bettmann, 38; Hulton
Archive, 39 top, 39 bottom, 40 top, 40 bottom; Collections of Henry Ford Museum and Greenfield Village, 41 top;
AP/Wide World Photos, 41 bottom; Corbis/Bettmann, 42 top; Corbis/Kevin Fleming, 42 bottom; Hulton Archive, 43.

Printed in the United States of America

1 2 3 4 5 6 7 8 9 06 05 04 03 02

TABLE of CONTENTS

Words that appear in the glossary are printed in **boldface**
type the first time they occur in the text.

CHAPTER 1

AN INDUSTRIAL GIANT

In the late 1800s, most people traveled by means of horse and carriage.

When Henry Ford was a boy, horses and wagons rolled down America's streets, and trains carried passengers over long distances. By the time Ford died in 1947, he had changed how the world traveled.

AN AMAZING MIND

Although not well educated, Ford had a sharp mind when it came to engineering. In his workshop in Detroit, Michigan, Ford built a car powered by a gas engine. Other inventors had already developed four-wheeled vehicles powered by gas, steam, and electricity, but after building his first successful car in 1896, Ford eventually changed the auto industry. He designed reliable, easy-to-operate cars that almost anyone could afford to buy.

The car that made Ford famous was the Model T, which appeared in 1908. For years, it was the only car he sold, and it became the most popular auto in the world. Ford's greatest achievement, however, was not the car itself, but the assembly-line method he created to produce it. In 1913, Ford perfected mass production. Other factory owners had tried moving parts through a factory, so workers spent less time moving around. Ford took this idea and went one step further, giving each worker just a few simple tasks to do over and over each day. Mass production cut down on the time it took to make a Model T. Workers were able to produce more cars each day, and Ford was able to cut his prices. The techniques of mass production spread to other auto companies, then to other industries. Ford's search for speed changed how the world worked.

With the fortune he made selling cars, Ford expanded into other businesses. At different times, his company made planes and boats, ran radio stations, owned coal mines and timberlands, and ran its own rubber plantation. Ford created a business empire and became perhaps the richest man in the world. Still, money was not the most important thing in Ford's life. He enjoyed what his wealth brought him, but he also spent his money to

Henry Ford posing in 1924 with his quadricycle and the 10 millionth Model T that rolled off the production lines

help others. Even though he helped create the modern industrial world, Ford had strong feelings for working people, such as farmers, and simple ways of living.

AN IMPERFECT MAN

Ford could also show **prejudice**, however, especially against Jews. He was criticized after a newspaper he owned repeatedly attacked Jews. At times, Ford also had a strained relationship with his workers. Ford revolutionized industry in 1914 when he began paying workers $5 a day—huge wages for the time. People flocked to Detroit, hoping to work for Ford. Years later, however, he resisted his employees' efforts to join **unions**. He always thought he knew what was best for his workers and tried to shape their lives outside the factory as well as inside.

Despite his flaws and his complex nature, many people knew and respected Ford as a great industrialist. His prejudice and ignorance could not take away from the contributions he made to modern society. Today, people know Ford's name because the company he founded still makes cars and trucks. In his lifetime, however, Ford was more than a businessman. When Ford died, a Detroit newspaper wrote, "Ford established a new age— it might also be said a new civilization." More than any other single person, Ford made the United States a country that relies on—and enjoys—the automobile.

Ford was a true visionary but also a controversial figure.

EARLY TALENTS

William and Mary Ford were not the richest people in Dearborn, Michigan, but their farm let them live comfortably. William had come to America from Ireland, looking for cheap land. Soon he owned more than 100 acres (41 hectares).

Henry's parents, William and Mary Ford

On July 30, 1863, he and Mary had a son and named him Henry. As a boy, Henry saw the hard work needed to run the family farm. He grew up thinking that machines, not people and horses, should do more of the work. That idea stayed with Henry throughout his life.

Henry showed an early curiosity about mechanical things and how they worked. His sister Margaret recalled that she and the rest of the Fords tried to keep wind-up toys from Henry because "he just takes them apart!" When Henry was about ten, he and some classmates built a small mill using a tiny waterwheel, a coffee grinder, and a rake. They used their invention to grind potatoes, clay, and pebbles. Later, the boys built a small steam engine. The engine exploded, and a bit of metal went through Henry's lip. Still, this accident did not keep Henry from exploring mechanical devices.

A STEAM-POWERED MARVEL

In 1876, just before his thirteenth birthday, Henry and his father traveled to Detroit. Ahead in the road, Henry saw a small vehicle running under its own steam power. Steam engines were sometimes used to power farm tools, such as saws. Farmers generally used horses to move the carts that carried the engines. This vehicle, however, was a "road engine"—the steam

Henry Ford at age two and a half

The Wisdom of Mrs. Ford

Mary Ford had a great influence on her son Henry. In 1876, when Henry was thirteen, he was deeply saddened when she died due to complications brought on during childbirth. Later in his life, Henry told a reporter what he learned from his mother.

She taught me that disagreeable jobs call for courage and patience, and self-discipline, and she also taught me that "I don't want to" gets a fellow nowhere…. My mother used to say, when I grumbled about it, "Life will give you many unpleasant tasks to do; your duty will be hard and disagreeable and painful to you at times, but you must do it. You may have pity on others, but you must not pity yourself. Do what you find to do, and what you know you must do, to the best of your ability."

When Ford was a teenager, some vehicles, including this fire engine, used power generated by steam engines.

engine was connected to the wheels of the cart. The engine used its own power to move along the road, while the farmer shoveled in coal to keep the engine running.

Henry ran over to talk to the man running the road engine. "It was the first vehicle other than horse-drawn that I had ever seen," Henry later wrote. The engineer explained how the vehicle worked, and later he let Henry run the engine. "It was that engine," Henry recalled, "which took me into automotive transportation."

Detroit, Michigan, in the 1890s

ON TO DETROIT

As Henry grew older, his father hoped he would take over the family farm. Henry, however, had other plans. When he was sixteen, Henry went to Detroit to look for a job and learn more about machines. In his spare time, Henry repaired watches and read magazines about science and mechanics.

One important article Henry read was about an engine powered by gasoline—the **internal combustion engine.** A French inventor named Étienne Lenoir made the first internal combustion engine in 1859, and German engineer Nikolaus Otto patented an improved gas engine in 1877. Henry, however, was still more interested in steam engines, which used coal or wood to boil water and create steam. This steam then turned the engine's **piston**, which created power. The gas engine, Henry thought, "was interesting to me only as all machinery was interesting." Years later, however, Henry found new appeal in the gas engine.

BUILDING A "HORSELESS CARRIAGE"

Late in 1880, Ford took a job at the Detroit Drydock Company, the largest shipbuilder in Detroit. When Henry left Detroit Drydock two years later, he was an expert in steam engines. Back on the family farm, Henry worked for the Westinghouse Company, which made road engines. Henry repaired and ran the engines for farmers in southern Michigan.

During this time, Henry thought about building a steam-powered "horseless carriage." Henry later wrote, "People had been talking about carriages without horses . . . ever since the steam engine was invented." The steam engine had been perfected about a century earlier, when Scotsman James Watt improved on a design created by Thomas Newcomen, an Englishman. As early as 1769, a French inventor named Nicolas Cugnot had invented a three-wheeled road vehicle that ran on steam. True steam-powered cars, however, did not appear until the 1880s.

Henry's first idea was to build a steam-powered tractor for farmers, not a vehicle for driving on roads.

Henry Ford at age twenty-three, a young man full of innovative ideas

Slowly, however, Henry realized steam engines were too dangerous for the invention he wanted to build. The boiler could explode, just as his childhood steam engine had. Henry began to consider the gasoline engine as a better power source for any vehicle he built. Other inventors shared this idea. In 1885, German inventor Gottlieb Daimler received a **patent** for a gas-powered motorcycle. Meanwhile, another German, Karl Benz, was developing a three-wheeled vehicle that is today called the first gas-powered car. The internal combustion engine was making its mark on transportation, and Henry hoped to do the same.

FORD'S FIRST GAS ENGINES

While living on his father's farm, Henry met his wife, Clara Jane Bryant. They married in 1888. About a year before the wedding, Mr. Ford told Henry he would give him his own farm—if Henry agreed to forget about engineering and stay on the farm. Henry said yes, but in the back of his mind he knew he would not be able to keep this promise.

Clara Bryant Ford in 1888, the year she and Henry were married

Inside a replica of Henry Ford's workshop in Detroit where he tinkered with his remarkable inventions

Henry Ford often used the bicycle—a relatively new contraption at the time—in his mechanical developments.

During the first years of his marriage, Henry spent his free time in his workshop, experimenting with the parts needed to build a gas engine. He wanted to put a small engine on a bicycle. At this time, bicycles, like gas engines, were relatively new inventions. The people who hoped to build a horseless carriage studied the developments being made in the bicycle industry. Henry's early gas engine, however, was too heavy to power a bicycle.

In September 1891, Ford returned to Detroit to work for the Edison Illuminating Company, Detroit's electric company. He hoped to learn more about electricity, since he believed it would be useful for powering horseless carriages. He set up another workshop and began building another gas engine. This one had a single **cylinder**, the metal chamber where the gas and air were mixed. Electricity provided the spark that exploded

the mixture and created the power that moved a piston inside the cylinder. "Every night . . . I worked on the new motor. I cannot say it was hard work. No work with interest is ever hard." Finally, in 1893, Ford was ready to test this engine.

An 1892 group of Edison Illuminating Company employees, including Henry Ford (back row, third from right)

The Power of Curiosity

In his autobiography, *My Life and Work*, Ford described the value of studying machines and how their parts interact:

There is an immense amount to be learned simply by tinkering with things. It is not possible to learn from books how everything is made—and a real mechanic ought to know how everything is made. Machines are to a mechanic what books are to a writer. He gets ideas from them, and if he has any brains he will apply those ideas.

CHAPTER 3

FROM "QUADRICYCLES" TO RACE CARS

On Christmas Eve, 1893, Clara Ford bustled around her kitchen preparing the family's Christmas meal, as her husband dragged his finished gas engine into the room. The Fords' baby son, Edsel, slept nearby. Ford had made the engine from scrap metal and parts of old machines. He needed his wife's help to test the engine. She had to drip fuel into it as Ford turned the flywheel. This wheel sucked air and fuel into the cylinder.

To start the explosion, Ford created a spark using the house's electrical current. When he connected into the electric line, the kitchen light dimmed. Suddenly, with a burst of smoke and flames, the engine came to life. "I didn't stop to play with it," Ford later said. He was already thinking about building a better engine.

Around the same time Ford built his test engine, he met Charles B. King, another inventor interested in horseless carriages. Gas-powered cars were still new in the United States—the first one had hit the roads earlier in 1893, after their perfection in Europe. King was working on engines with four cylinders— more cylinders meant more power. He worked through 1894 and 1895 on his design and took his first road test on March 6, 1896, as Ford rode along on his bicycle. A Detroit newspaper wrote, "The first horseless carriage seen in this city was out on the streets last night." By now, Ford was almost ready to test his own four-wheeled vehicle, which he had been working on with friends since 1895.

Edsel Ford in 1898

THE QUADRICYCLE

Ford called his first car a "quadricycle," meaning "four wheels." This automobile—as horseless carriages were now sometimes called—had four rubber bicycle wheels and an iron frame, but many parts were made of wood. Its two-cylinder engine produced a top speed of about 20 miles (32.2 kilometers) per hour. The quadricycle weighed about 500 pounds (227 kilograms), less than half the weight of King's car, and much less than most horseless carriages. Throughout his career, Ford tried to make his cars as light as possible.

Henry Ford with his quadricycle outside his workshop in 1896

Ford prepared to test his car on June 4, 1896. First he had to take down part of the brick wall of his workshop because his car was too wide to fit through the building's door. Once outside the workshop, Ford drove the car a short distance, but soon the quadricycle stopped. With the help of an assistant, Ford quickly got the car running again and finished his short test-drive around the neighborhood.

In the weeks that followed, Ford drove his car through the streets of Detroit. "It was considered to be something of a nuisance," he later wrote, "for it made a racket and it scared horses." Once, Ford drove out to his father's farm and offered to take him for a ride. Mr. Ford, however, like many people of the era, was suspicious of this new invention. Slightly disappointed with his father's reaction, Ford returned to Detroit to keep working on his car.

Other Automakers of the Day

While Ford worked on his first cars in Detroit, other U.S. inventors designed and built their own cars. Frank and Charles Duryea, who had built the first gas-powered car in the United States, sold their first car early in 1896. Ransom Olds, who had started out building steam engines for vehicles, switched to gas engines and started designing a car that was later called the Oldsmobile (an 1896 model is shown above). Another successful carmaker of the day was Alexander Winton, the racer. In Connecticut, Alexander Pope, a bicycle manufacturer, began producing both gas and electric-powered cars. Despite all this activity, only about 4,000 cars were made in the United States in 1900.

Ford did not plan to sell his quadricycle. To him, it was merely an experiment. Yet when someone offered him $200 for the car, he took it. Ford was now a professional automaker—if only in a small way. He planned to build more cars and sell these as well. He began working on an improved quadricycle, and some local investors gave him money to start a company. Ford worked slowly, trying out different designs. The investors thought he was taking too much time, and they ended their deal with Ford. Throughout his career, Ford would have difficulty working with investors and business partners.

By 1899, Ford was ready to manufacture a new car. He left his job at the Edison Company, found new investors, and opened the Detroit Automobile Company. In 1900, the company introduced its first vehicle—a delivery wagon. Ford took a local journalist on a test-drive. The reporter wrote that the wagon, "this newest and most perfect of forces ... flew along with the poetry of motion."

In 1899, Ford opened the Detroit Automobile Company.

Despite this positive review, Ford's company soon closed. His early vehicles were not as well made as some of his competitors' cars. He wanted to improve his cars and needed more time than his investors wanted to give him. Ford, however, was soon back at work building new vehicles. He moved from delivery wagons to race cars.

The 999 racer with driver Barney Oldfield in 1902

The first race cars had appeared almost as soon as inventors created the first horseless carriages. The engineering that went into race cars helped improve all cars, and the races themselves stirred public interest in the auto. Ford decided to enter racing to show off his car-building skills. He made a car that reached about 60 miles (96.5 km) per hour, and on October 10, 1901, he entered his first race.

Only two drivers competed in the day's last and most important event. Ford went against Alexander Winton, a champion racer known for his fast, powerful cars. Winton took an early lead, but when mechanical troubles forced him to slow down, Ford shot past him to win the race.

From then on, Ford stuck to designing race cars and let others drive them. One car, nicknamed the "999," was the largest automobile Ford had ever built. It was nearly 10 feet (3 meters) long and used a four-cylinder engine. In its first race, the 999 set a new U.S. speed record for a 5-mile (8-km) race, covering the course in a little over five minutes. "The 999 did what it was intended to," Ford wrote. "It advertised the fact that I could build a fast motor car." Ford was now one of the leading automakers in Detroit, which was becoming a center for car manufacturing. Once again, Ford was ready to start a car company.

A Wild Race

After Henry Ford won his first and only auto race in 1901, his wife Clara wrote a letter to her brother describing the event.

I wish you could have seen him. Also have heard the cheering when he passed Winton. The people went wild. One man threw his hat up, and when it came down he stamped on it, he was so excited. Another man had to hit his wife on the head to keep her from going off the handle. She stood up in her seat and screamed, "I'd bet fifty dollars on Ford if I had it." They were friends of ours.

Even before racing the 999, Ford had found a new partner to invest in his cars. He also hired a new shop assistant and business manager. Then Ford made a deal with John and Horace Dodge, two of the best machinists in Detroit, to provide the engine for his new car. Other suppliers provided the body, tires, and wheels. By July 1903, Ford's new business—the Ford Motor Company—sold its first car, which Ford called the Model A. "The cars gained a reputation for standing up," Ford wrote in his autobiography. "They were tough, they were simple, and they were well made."

At the beginning, Ford's company produced several cars a day, but within two years they were up to twenty-five cars a day. Parts came into Ford's small shop from other companies, and his workers hand-assembled them into cars. During the first year, Ford and other executives sometimes worked sixteen hours a day, seven days a week. Ford spent most of his time in the experiment room, constantly trying to improve his car. His efforts paid off, and he made at least $150 profit on every car he sold. Ford's business was a success.

Over time, the company made slight changes to the Model A, or introduced new models. Each of these was also named with a letter of the alphabet, and soon the Model S was on the road. Still, Ford was not completely happy. Earlier he had told an employee, "The proper system, as I have it in mind, is to get the car to the multitude." For most Americans, cars were still a luxury. Ford's new car would change that.

Horace Dodge, along with his brother John, played an important role in the Ford automobile business.

As head of the Ford Motor Company in 1904

Employees of the Ford Motor Company in 1903

THE UNIVERSAL CAR

Ford called his dream auto "the universal car," since everyone would be able to afford one. He had been thinking about this car for years. He wanted it to be light, easy to operate, and easy to fix. One way to keep the car simple was to use as few parts as possible. The Model T

The Model T proved to be a popular car throughout the United States.

became Ford's universal car, and he was sure it would be a hit with buyers. "It had to be," he wrote. "There was no way it could escape being so, for it had not been made in a day." All of Ford's car-making experience and the knowledge of his engineers went into building the Model T, which Ford introduced in 1908.

Ford soon learned that he was right about the Model T and its appeal to Americans. Although the company still sold some of its older models, the T became its best-seller. The first year the Model T was available, Ford sold more than 10,000. Soon Ford decided he would sell only the Model T. With that car, Ford declared, he would "democratize" the automobile. "When I'm through," he said, "everybody will be able to afford one. . . . The horse will have disappeared from our highways, the automobile will be taken for granted and there won't be any problems."

TAKING ON ALAM

Ford, however, had his own problems during this period. For several years, his company had been under a legal cloud. A group of car manufacturers called the Association of Licensed Automobile Manufacturers (ALAM) claimed it owned a patent on gas-powered cars. Anyone selling a car had to pay ALAM a fee or face a lawsuit. Ford had always refused to pay the fee. The gas-powered car, he argued, had been created by many different people.

"The World Is Ford's"

To stir interest in cars, Ford and other automakers touted their products in newspapers and magazine ads. Here is part of an early Ford ad.

The Ford Line for 1908

As per usual—will eclipse everything else . . .

There'll be one new runabout—a light roadster that will show the way to everything else on wheels, quality, price, performance, and appearance beyond compare.

Two other surprises—yes, a light touring car is one of them—that will be the delight of prospective buyers, the despair of competition.

. . . You'll say "the world is Ford's for 1908."

Of all the smaller car manufacturers, only Ford kept fighting ALAM, and the group sued him. In 1909, ALAM won the case, but Ford appealed the decision. A Detroit newspaper praised him as a "man of backbone." Ford won the appeal and kept his independence. Throughout his career, Ford kept fighting to run his company the way he wanted.

MASS PRODUCTION

As demand for the Model T rose, Ford built a bigger plant. By 1911, the Ford Motor Company had more than 4,000 employees—double what it had in 1908. This workforce turned out 35,000 cars a year—almost six times as many as the company produced in 1908. Ford was learning how to build cars faster and cheaper, but he continued to look for new ways to improve his manufacturing. His greatest business accomplishment was perfecting mass production.

Ford had to build a bigger plant as demand for the Model T increased.

Mass production defined industry during the twentieth century. It used machines to bring parts to workers, who then performed one or two simple tasks over and over. The speed of the machines and the repetition of the work meant fewer workers could produce more products in a shorter period of time. These improvements meant companies could charge less for their goods. Henry Ford did not invent mass production, but he assembled the pieces that made it work.

Eli Whitney began using interchangeable parts in the manufacture of guns in 1798.

For mass production to work, every sample of a particular part must be exactly the same, or interchangeable. Before the Industrial Revolution of the late eighteenth century, craftsmen made parts for most mechanical items by hand. The parts differed slightly from one another, even when the same worker made them. Then, in 1798, Eli Whitney planned to use machines to make guns, so the parts for each gun would be identical. The French government had begun using this method of production several decades earlier. Whitney's plan was too ambitious. He promised to make 10,000 guns in two years, but he could not pull it off. The perfection of **interchangeable parts** in gun manufacturing came about twenty years later.

Workers on the assembly line inside the Ford Motor Company plant in Dearborn, Michigan

While Whitney was thinking of building better guns, a mill owner named Oliver Evans began using steam engines to power large belts called **conveyor belts**. The belts moved grain through his mill. Evans's belts helped shape the idea of the assembly line. Later, meatpackers used belts to move cows and hogs through their processing plants.

Just one day's production
of Model Ts in 1913

At his plant, Ford already used interchangeable parts. He also saw the value of moving parts along a belt to bring them to the workers. Then he added something new—each worker did just a specific task during the assembly process. Before mass production, one worker might build an entire component of a car. With mass production, several employees split up the work, and the component moved from one worker to the next along a belt.

Ford did not create this new system on his own. Different workers made suggestions and tried out new ideas. Ford, however, quickly saw the value of mass production and introduced it in 1913. Afterward, he kept looking for ways to improve it. Mass production drastically reduced the time it took to assemble the different parts of a car. Soon Ford's plant was producing twice as many Model T's using the same number of workers. The price of the Model T began to fall, and Ford's "universal car" was a reality.

Mass Production in Place

In his autobiography, Henry Ford describes mass production at his plant.

Some men do only one or two small operations, others do more. The man who places a part does not fasten it—the part may not be fully in place until after several operations later. The man who puts in a bolt does not put on the nut; the man who puts on the nut does not tighten it. . . . Every piece of work in the shop moves . . . the point is that there is no lifting or trucking anything other than materials.

Ford's new methods of production shook the industrial world, as other factory owners borrowed his methods to lower their costs. Ford, however, was not done introducing new ways to run his business.

In 1914, Ford decided to pay almost all his factory workers at least $5 per day and to cut the workday to eight hours, six days a week. Although $5 a day seems very little now, it was a huge salary for an industrial worker at that time. Until 1914, the average Ford worker earned less than $2.50 per day, and wages were even lower in other industries. In his autobiography, Ford wrote, "It ought to be the employer's ambition, as a leader, to pay better wages than any similar line of business."

The pay raise stirred controversy. One New York newspaper praised Ford for "a magnificent act of generosity." Another said Ford had committed "economic blunders, if not crimes" that would hurt all of America. Workers across the country welcomed the news of the pay raise, hoping that one day they would see a similar raise, while other carmakers and business leaders worried they could not afford to match Ford. Some wondered if Ford could stay in business paying such high wages.

In 1914, workers gathered to hear the remarkable announcement of a $5-a-day wage.

Ford could afford it because mass production had increased his profits. He also tied part of the $5-per-day salary to a bonus that workers received depending on future profits Ford made. Ford's decision also made sense for his company. The higher wage would earn loyalty from his workers. Also, higher pay meant more Ford workers could afford Model T's. As wages went up at other companies, these workers would also be able to buy Ford's cars.

TOTAL CONTROL

Along with the raise, Ford added another new element to his workplace. He created a department to watch over Ford workers outside the factory. Many of the workers were immigrants who spoke little or no English. Others were illiterate. The company now helped with workers' education, health, and living conditions. Ford said, "We want to make men in this factory as well as automobiles."

Ford thought he was doing his workers a favor and making them better citizens. He also expected his employees to follow all his rules—at work and at home. Still, some workers and some people outside Ford did not like the company's efforts to become involved in every part of his workers' lives.

An English class for Ford employees

Ford also expected his employees to work hard. Company officials timed how long it took to perform certain jobs and build certain items. Workers had to meet strict standards. Some workers nicknamed Ford "the speed-up king" and grumbled about the fast pace in the factory. One woman wrote to the company about her husband, who came home from the Ford plant "so done out," he was too tired to eat supper. "That $5 a day is a blessing . . ." she wrote, "but oh they earn it."

The Peace Ship

In 1915, more than a year after the start of World War I (1914–1918), Henry Ford set off on a mission to end the war. Ford and other Americans feared the United States would be dragged into the war. Ford hired a ship so he could sail to Europe and ask the leaders there to end the war. The vessel was soon called the "Peace Ship," and it set sail on December 4 (left). Ford promised he would end the war by Christmas. Most newspapers thought he was **naïve** or just plain foolish to think he could stop the war.

The newspapers proved to be right. Ford's trip was a failure—one of the few at this point in his career. Afterward, Ford told a friend why he had tried to end the war. "I do not want the things money can buy. I want to live a life, to make the world a little better for [my] having lived in it."

Whatever problems Ford's workers had, they continued to make Model T's faster and cheaper than ever. In 1916, Ford sold more than 700,000 "Tin Lizzies," as the car was sometimes called. The cheap, reliable Model T gave Americans new mobility. They could live farther from their jobs and travel farther on vacations. Autos also required roads, gas, and repairs, and new industries sprang up to meet these needs.

The success of the Model T made Ford and the other **stockholders** in his company rich. Those profits were particularly important to Horace and John Dodge. These early suppliers to Ford also owned stock in the company. With their share of the profits, they started their own car company in 1914. This competition with Ford created problems.

The Dodges did not like some of Henry Ford's business decisions. They wanted Ford to pay higher **dividends**—money given to stockholders out of a company's profits. The Dodge brothers wanted to use their dividends to expand their own company. Ford, however, wanted to keep the profits to build a new plant on the River Rouge, near Dearborn.

The Dodges decided to sue Ford, and the case was not settled until 1919. The Ford Motor Company was ordered to pay a special dividend of about $19 million, with 10 percent of that going to the Dodges. By then,

Henry Ford ran for the U.S. Senate in 1918, but he was defeated.

Vote for
HENRY FORD
For Senator

The Workingman's Friend

Ford had decided he needed total control of his company to avoid future problems with other stockholders. He eventually spent more than $100 million to buy all the company's stock he did not already own. By July 1919, he was the sole owner of the Ford Motor Company.

MORE LEGAL TROUBLES

In 1918, Ford briefly stepped away from the auto business to pursue a new interest. The Democratic Party asked Ford to run for Michigan's seat in the U.S. Senate. Ford lost a close race, and he spent almost two years in court trying to overturn the results with a recount. The effort failed. (Ford briefly considered entering politics again in 1922, as a presidential candidate, but he changed his mind.)

During the time Ford was buying all the stock in his company, he was also involved in another lawsuit. This one, however, was personal. In 1916, the *Chicago Tribune* had called Ford "an ignorant idealist." Ford sued the newspaper for libel, or making a false statement against him. The case dragged on for years. In 1919, Ford appeared in court, and the opposing lawyer tried his best to show that Ford truly was ignorant.

Ford confused the American Revolution (1775–1783) with the War of 1812, and he could not answer other basic questions about American history. Finally Ford said, "I admit I am ignorant about most things." In the end, the jury agreed Ford had been libeled, but it awarded him just 6 cents for winning the case. Some Americans could not believe this industrial genius was so uneducated. Ford's public reputation fell a bit after the trial.

Ford also suffered from the articles published in a newspaper he owned. In 1918, Ford bought the *Dearborn Independent*. He used the paper to promote his ideas and his cars. Starting in 1920, Ford and the

The Ford International Weekly

THE DEARBORN INDEPENDENT

$1.50   Dearborn, Michigan, August 6, 1921   Ten Cents

And Now Leprosy Is Yielding to Science
Years of experimenting brings a remedy

Fountain Lake, the Home of John Muir
A story of naturalist's wilderness abode

Fighting the Devil in Modern Babylon
First of a series of articles on New York by Rev. Dr. John Roach Straton

Jewish Jazz—Moron Music—Becomes Our National Music
Story of "Popular Song" Control in the United States

The Chief Justices of the Supreme Court
Only ten men have held this post since the tribunal was first organized

Teaching the Deaf to Hear With Their Eyes
How Chicago is educating afflicted children

Many By-Products From Sweet Potatoes
Recent discoveries prove great possibilities

An issue of the
Dearborn Independent
from August 6, 1921

paper ran into trouble when some of its stories showed prejudice against Jews. Ford did not have a personal dislike of all Jewish people. His social circle included the leading rabbi in Detroit, and the company architect, Albert Kahn, was Jewish. Yet Ford seemed to accept the false idea that Jewish bankers controlled the world's economy, and the *Independent* often wrote about this notion. Ford's position as a leading industrialist seemed to give weight to this **propaganda**. After another lawsuit, Ford had to publicly apologize for his paper's **anti-Semitic** writings, though his thinking did not change. To some people, Ford's anti-Semitism was another example of how this successful man could be so ignorant in some matters.

The Rouge at Work

For many years, Charles Sorensen was in charge of production at the Ford Motor Company. In his autobiography, he describes the activity at the River Rouge plant.

By 1923 . . . the Ford conveyor system, which is responsible in great part for Ford quantity production, was developing in every direction. One could see with one's own eyes raw material being transformed into parts, parts into units, and units to the assembly line for the finished product. Solid carloads—even trainloads—of engines, front and rear axles, transmissions, radiators, and magnetos rolled out of the Rouge railroad yards to branch assemblies in other cities.

Ford's legal troubles did not affect the success of his car company. He went ahead with his plans for a new factory. "The Rouge," as it was called, grew into a sprawling industrial complex that covered 2,000 acres (810 ha) and employed 75,000 people. Apart from the Rouge, Ford also owned sawmills, iron and coal mines, railroads, and ships. He built his own small power plants and started a radio station and telegraph service. The Ford empire grew internationally as well. In Brazil, Ford bought land to start his own rubber plantation, and he opened plants as far away as Australia. Most of these projects were designed to increase profits within the main business of making cars. By controlling the raw materials that went into cars, Ford spent less money than if he bought finished products from other companies, a business concept known as vertical integration.

The River Rouge plant was an enormous facility that covered thousands of acres.

During this time, Ford made a few changes to the Model T and introduced new models. Still, the Model T remained a cheap and simple car, and during the 1920s it was the best-selling auto in the world. In 1927, however, change came to Ford and his company.

CHAPTER 6

DIFFICULT YEARS

Henry and Edsel Ford were proud to introduce the new Model A at the New York Industrial Expo in 1928.

opposite: Crowds of people in the Wall Street district reacting to the stock market crash in October 1929

Henry Ford did not want to change the Model T. Its success had made him famous and changed the world. But by 1926, some Ford officials knew the company could not produce the Model T much longer, as sales were starting to fall. Reluctantly, Ford agreed to replace his beloved car.

In May 1927, the Ford Motor Company produced its 15 millionth Model T. By the end of that year, the Tin Lizzie was gone, and Ford introduced a new Model A. This car had more power than the Model T and new safety features, yet it was still affordable. Ford spent more than $1 million to advertise the car, and the Model A was an immediate hit. By 1929, the Model A was the best-selling car in America.

The year 1929 was good for Ford, but it was not a good year for the U.S. economy. In October, the stock market crashed. Many Americans who had bought stocks in different companies saw the value of these stocks fall. Investors sometimes lost all their savings. While the 1920s had been a decade of great wealth for many, the United States was about to enter the worst economic period in its history. Ford and his company also felt the effects of this era, known as the **Great Depression**.

Giving Ford the Facts

Edsel Ford's brother-in-law, Ernest Kanzler, worked for the Ford Motor Company. In 1926, Kanzler wrote to Henry Ford, trying to convince him that the company had to replace the Model T. Here is part of his letter.

I can write certain things that I find it difficult to say to you. It is one of the handicaps of the power of your personality which perhaps you least of all realize, but most people when with you hesitate to say what they think. . . . We have not gone ahead in the last few years, have barely held our own, whereas competition has made great strides. You have always said you either go forward or backwards, you can't stand still. . . . Our Ford customers . . . are going to other manufacturers, and our best dealers are low in morale and not making the money they used to. . . . The best evidence that conditions are not right is the fact that with most of the bigger men in the organization there is a growing uneasiness because things are not right—they feel our position weakening and our grip slipping. . . . With every additional car our competitors sell they get stronger and we get weaker.

During the Great Depression, the hungry and the homeless gathered in breadlines throughout the United States.

BAD TIMES

Ford tried to prepare for the bad times that hit at the end of 1929. He thought he could help the company sell more cars by lowering prices. He also tried to help his workers by raising their pay. By 1931, however, the economy had grown worse, and Ford had to cut his employees' pay. Ford also laid off thousands of workers and shut down some assembly lines.

The bad times of the Great Depression seemed to bring out the worst in Ford. He made every effort to fight labor unions at his plant. The unions wanted better working conditions and higher pay for the workers. To Ford, unions were a threat to running his business the way he wanted. He also believed he took good care of his workers. "I think we have made better bargains for them," Ford wrote, "than any . . . they could make for themselves."

During the Great Depression, many Americans lost their jobs and their homes and struggled with hunger. For people lucky enough to have jobs, unions seemed to offer hope for a better life. Some Americans sought even bigger changes than those the unions wanted. Some of these people joined the Communist Party. The

Communists wanted a socialist economy in which the government would take over the operation of most companies. The U.S. Communists were connected with the Communist Party in the Soviet Union, where a revolution in 1917 had established a socialist economy. Socialists abroad and in the United States thought that **capitalism**, the American economic system, hurt workers.

Not everyone who supported socialism in the United States joined the U.S. Communist Party; other political parties also opposed capitalism. Most Americans did not accept socialism at all, but the Great Depression did encourage many people to try to improve the U.S. economic system. Unions were one of those options.

TROUBLE IN DEARBORN

As one of the most powerful leaders in American business, Ford was often criticized by Communists and union leaders alike. In 1932, some Communists organized a protest at the Rouge. Local police tried to stop the march, using tear gas and clubs. The protesters fought back with rocks or any other weapons they could find. Security guards from River Rouge also took part, spraying the crowd with fire hoses. Finally, some police officers fired into the crowd, killing four protesters.

A few days later, about 15,000 people attended the funeral of the four dead protesters. Some Ford employees went to the funeral, and they lost their jobs soon afterward. Apparently Ford had sent loyal workers to the funeral to find out which Ford employees supported the protesters. This incident and others during the 1930s showed that Ford often placed his company's interests over those of his workers. The man once praised for introducing the $5 wage was now sometimes seen as an enemy of the working people.

Despite the troubles caused by the Great Depression, Ford kept trying to build better cars. In 1932, he introduced his first eight-cylinder engine. Other carmakers were using six-cylinder engines, and Ford wanted something more powerful. The design of Ford's engine had two sets of four cylinders placed at an angle forming a "V," so the engine was called a V-8.

Other carmakers had built V-8 engines before but only to power expensive cars. Ford, as always, wanted a product most Americans could afford. The effort to make a cheaper V-8 was expensive, but Ford didn't care. He told production manager Charles Sorensen, "Charlie, we have too much money in the bank.... Let's you and me pull that down."

Ford and his company spent three years perfecting the new engine. When it finally hit the road, the public loved the V-8's extra power. The engine needed some improvements, but the Ford Motor Company used the basic design of its V-8 for more than twenty years.

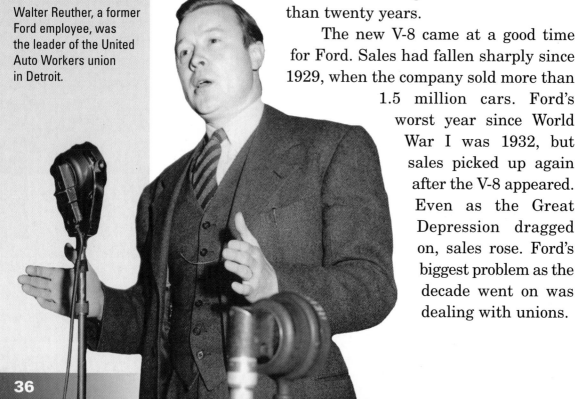

Walter Reuther, a former Ford employee, was the leader of the United Auto Workers union in Detroit.

The new V-8 came at a good time for Ford. Sales had fallen sharply since 1929, when the company sold more than 1.5 million cars. Ford's worst year since World War I was 1932, but sales picked up again after the V-8 appeared. Even as the Great Depression dragged on, sales rose. Ford's biggest problem as the decade went on was dealing with unions.

A UNION SHOP

In 1935, the U.S. government gave workers the legal right to form unions. Ford, however, still resisted unions. The other major carmakers made deals with the United Auto Workers (UAW) union in 1937, but Ford refused to go along. Walter Reuther, a former Ford employee, led the UAW in Detroit. He tried to recruit union workers at River Rouge, but Ford's security force beat him and three other union officials. After the attack, the guards dumped Reuther and the others down a steel staircase. Many newspapers criticized this violence against the union leaders.

Ford believed most people opposed the UAW. Still, the law was clear—Ford workers had the right to join a union. After a long court battle, the UAW and the Ford Motor Company reached an agreement in 1941. Ford could not believe his workers would oppose him and join the union. "He had been certain," Charlie Sorensen later wrote, "that Ford workers would stand by him. . . . He never was the same after that."

Many of Ford Motor Company workers went on strike during the struggle between Ford and the labor unions.

Protest at The Rouge

Here is part of a news article from the *New York Times* on the 1932 protest at Ford's plant.

The demonstration by the unemployed, who had planned to ask Ford company officials, through a committee, to give them work, started quietly, but before it was over Dearborn pavements were stained with blood, streets were littered with broken glass and the wreckage of bullet-ridden automobiles, and nearly every window in the Ford plant's employment building had been broken. . . .

Carrying banners and signs demanding jobs, the demonstrators marched in orderly fashion . . . to the Dearborn city limits.

There they encountered a squad of Dearborn police, who warned them to turn back to Detroit.

Ignoring the warning, the marchers surged over the city lines, and instantly the fighting broke out. . . .

Dodging the missiles [thrown by the marchers] the police drew their guns, pointing them threateningly at the angry mob. . . .

The demonstrators had just made their request for a hearing in the [Ford] employment office, when someone started to shoot. The report of the pistol shot started a general melee. Hand-to-hand fighting began. . . .

Men fell with gunshot wounds in their legs and were carried out of further harm's way by their comrades, who tried to commandeer automobiles to take the wounded away. When automobile drivers refused to help, their cars were stoned.

REACHING AN END

Union troubles were not Ford's only problems during the late 1930s. In 1938, he suffered a stroke. At age seventy-five, Ford still ran the company, even though Edsel was president. The stroke, however, reminded others that Ford was getting old, and his health became more of a concern during the next few years.

A worldwide problem of the day was the growing trouble in Europe. Adolf Hitler, the Nazi leader of Germany, rebuilt his country's army during the 1930s, planning to expand his country's borders. Once again, Ford did not want

As Henry Ford grew older, more of the company's responsibilities fell to his son, Edsel.

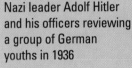

Nazi leader Adolf Hitler and his officers reviewing a group of German youths in 1936

Workers assembling the nose of a bomber plane at Ford's Willow Run plant in 1942

Henry and Clara Ford with their grandson Henry II in the mid-1940s

the United States involved in another world war, which started in 1939. Germany launched a surprise attack on Poland, and Great Britain and France aided the Poles. Despite his feelings about the war, Ford agreed to help the U.S. government build airplane engines. He also built a new factory, called Willow Run, to produce bomber planes.

Willow Run was another huge complex. More than a half mile (0.8 km) long, it could hold 70,000 workers. Ford began making bombers there in May 1942, five months after the Japanese attacked Pearl Harbor, Hawaii, and the United States entered World War II. Many U.S. industries made weapons and supplies for the military. Most used the methods of mass production Ford had perfected for the Model T.

DIFFICULT TIMES

The work at Willow Run began slowly. Ford could not meet the U.S. Army's goal of 405 planes per month until 1944. The company, however, aided the war effort in many other ways, building trucks, jeeps, and glider planes.

During the war, Ford suffered a tremendous personal loss. His son, Edsel, died in May 1943. As Ford had grown older and more unpredictable, Edsel had tried to explain his father's actions to others. People outside the company found it much easier to deal with Edsel than with his father. Yet Ford had sometimes treated his son badly and refused to give him true power in the company.

After Edsel's death, and since Ford's health was worsening after a second stroke, people wondered who would run the Ford Motor Company. Finally, Edsel's son, Henry Ford II, stepped forward. Ford did not want Henry II in charge, but in September 1945, his grandson took full control. Ford was bitter about the change, but he knew he was too old and sick to stop it.

Everyday Work

In his autobiography, Henry Ford outlined some of his ideas about life and work.

Every advance begins in a small way and with the individual. The mass can be no better than the sum of the individuals. Advancement begins within the man himself; when he advances from half-interest to strength of purpose; when he advances from hesitancy to decisive directness; when he advances from immaturity to maturity of judgment . . . why, then the world advances! The advance is not easy. We live in flabby times when men are being taught that everything ought to be easy. Work that amounts to anything will never be easy. . . . It is not work that men object to, but the element of drudgery. We must drive out drudgery wherever we find it. We shall never be wholly civilized until we remove the treadmill from the daily job.

FORD'S LAST YEARS

As Henry II took over, the Ford Motor Company faced difficult times. Many workers did not like the way the company had been run since Edsel's death, and the company was losing money. Henry II fired some old managers and brought in new ones. These new leaders were nicknamed the "Whiz Kids," and they helped Ford grow stronger. Henry Ford had to admit that his grandson was doing a good job with the company. "I guess young Henry knows what he's doing," Ford said.

In their later years, Henry and Clara Ford enjoyed bird-watching and spending time at home.

Henry Ford II proved to be a good leader of the Ford Motor Company.

Thousands of people watched Henry Ford's funeral procession in 1947.

The work of Henry Ford helped Detroit become the modern city it is today.

The elder Ford, however, was not always so clear in what he was doing. His advanced age and his strokes left him confused at times. He believed he had enemies who wanted to harm him, and he often spent time alone. Still, sometimes Ford had good days when he thought clearly and enjoyed being with others. His last good day was April 7, 1947.

Ford took a drive that afternoon, then settled in for a quiet evening at home. In bed that night, he had trouble sleeping and began to cough. His wife, Clara, called for a doctor. Before the doctor arrived, Henry Ford was

Thanks to Henry Ford, people began using cars as a part of everyday life.

dead from a cerebral hemorrhage—bleeding in the brain.

At Ford's funeral, thousands of people stood in the rain to honor the great automobile pioneer. President Harry Truman sent a note, and great business leaders praised Ford's accomplishments. Newspapers across the country described his great contributions to the world. Besides his automotive advances, Ford also gave huge sums of money through the Ford Foundation. Although Ford had many flaws, on the days after his death he was remembered as a hero. With his Model T and mass production, Ford helped shape the modern world.

Remembering Ford

Here is part of an article from the *Detroit News*, written shortly after Henry Ford's death.

No other man ever so changed the face of the world in his lifetime as did Henry Ford. . . . He released his countrymen and people everywhere from the older restrictions of locality. . . . To place in the reach of the greatest number of people a useful product which would lift the whole level of living was . . . a purpose to which he committed a boundless originality and inexhaustible energy.

TIMELINE

1863	Henry Ford is born on July 30 in Dearborn, Michigan
1879	Works in Detroit machine shops
1888	Marries Clara Bryant and settles in Dearborn
1891	Begins working at the Edison Illuminating Company, Detroit
1893	Builds and tests his own internal combustion engine
1896	Tests his first car, the Quadricycle
1899	Becomes a partner in the Detroit Automobile Company
1901	Wins his first automobile race
1903	Forms the Ford Motor Company with a small group of investors; sells first Model A
1908	Introduces the Model T
1913	Uses the first automotive assembly line
1914	Announces a wage of $5 per day for most Ford Motor Company employees
1915	Sails for Europe on the "Peace Ship"
1918	Loses race for U.S. Senate
1919	Loses lawsuit brought by Horace and John Dodge; takes complete control of the Ford Motor Company
1927	Ends production of the Model T and introduces new Model A
1932	Produces a V-8 engine for the Model A; a protest outside River Rouge ends in four deaths
1937	Tries to keep unions out of his plants
1941	Signs an agreement with the United Auto Workers Union
1947	Dies at age eighty-three on April 7

anti-Semitic: having a prejudice against Jews as a religious or racial group

capitalism: an economic system in which private citizens own most businesses

communists: members of a political party who support a government that is controlled by a single party and that owns all businesses

conveyor belts: motorized belts that move items through a factory

cylinder: part of a gas engine where air and fuel are ignited to create a small explosion and move the piston

dividends: money paid to stockholders in a company from profits the company earns

Great Depression: a period in U.S. history (1929 through the early 1940s) marked by widespread poverty and unemployment

interchangeable parts: identical machine-made parts used to make various products

internal combustion engine: an engine powered by igniting a mixture of air and gasoline

naïve: lacking experience and liable to be too trusting

patent: a legal document that gives inventors ownership of their inventions

piston: a round metal rod that moves up and down in an engine's cylinder, creating the power that turns the wheels

prejudice: dislike for the members of a religious, racial, or ethnic group

propaganda: information deliberately spread to promote or hurt a person or organization

stockholders: investors who own part of a company

unions: groups that represent workers in a particular industry, seeking better wages and working conditions

TO FIND OUT MORE

BOOKS

Gourley, Catherine. *Wheels of Time: A Biography of Henry Ford.* Brookfield, Conn.: Millbrook Press, 1997.

Harris, Jacqueline. *Henry Ford.* New York: Franklin Watts, 1984.

Italia, Robert. *Great Automakers and Their Cars.* Minneapolis: Oliver Press, 1993.

Joseph, Paul. *Henry Ford.* Edina, Minn.: Abdo Publishing, 1996.

Malam, John. *Henry Ford: An Authorized Biography.* Chicago: Heinemann Library, 2001.

INTERNET SITES

Driving Force: Henry Ford
http://www.time.com/time/time100/builder/profile/ford.html
Time magazine's profile of Ford as one of the most important businessmen of the twentieth century.

Henry Ford and the Model T
http://www.wiley.com/products/subject/business/forbes/ford.html
Highlights Ford's accomplishments.

The Life of Henry Ford
http://www.hfmgv.org/histories/hf/henry.html
A biography from the Henry Ford Museum.

Model T Ford Club of America
http://www.mtca.com
Information about the Model T for collectors and the curious.

A Science Odyssey: People and Discoveries: Henry Ford
http://www.pbs.org/wgbh/aso/databank/entries/btford.html
A biography with a link to a more detailed discussion of the assembly line.

About the Author

As an editor at *Weekly Reader* for six years, **Michael Burgan** created educational material for an interactive online service and wrote on current events. Now a freelance author, Michael has written more than thirty books, primarily for children and young adults. These include biographies of Secretary of State Madeleine Albright, Presidents John Adams and John F. Kennedy, and astronaut John Glenn. His other historical writings include two volumes in the series *American Immigration* and the four-volume set *Cold War*. Michael has a bachelor of arts degree from the University of Connecticut and resides in that state.